DON'T FORGET
TO FEED THE
CAT!

PACKING LIST

BINOCULARS
RUCKSACK
WATER BOTTLE
MOSQUITO SPRAY
SHORTS
PENCILS   ← FOR US
JAM SANDWICH
BANANAS (LOTS)
    ↑
FOR
THEM

EXTRA SOCKS
SUNSCREEN
CAMERA
HIKING BOOTS
PILLOW
SLEEPING BAG
TOOTHBRUSH
PAJAMAS
COMB
COMPASS
TEDDY?

PASSPORT

TENT!

REMEMBER TO
CALL HOME

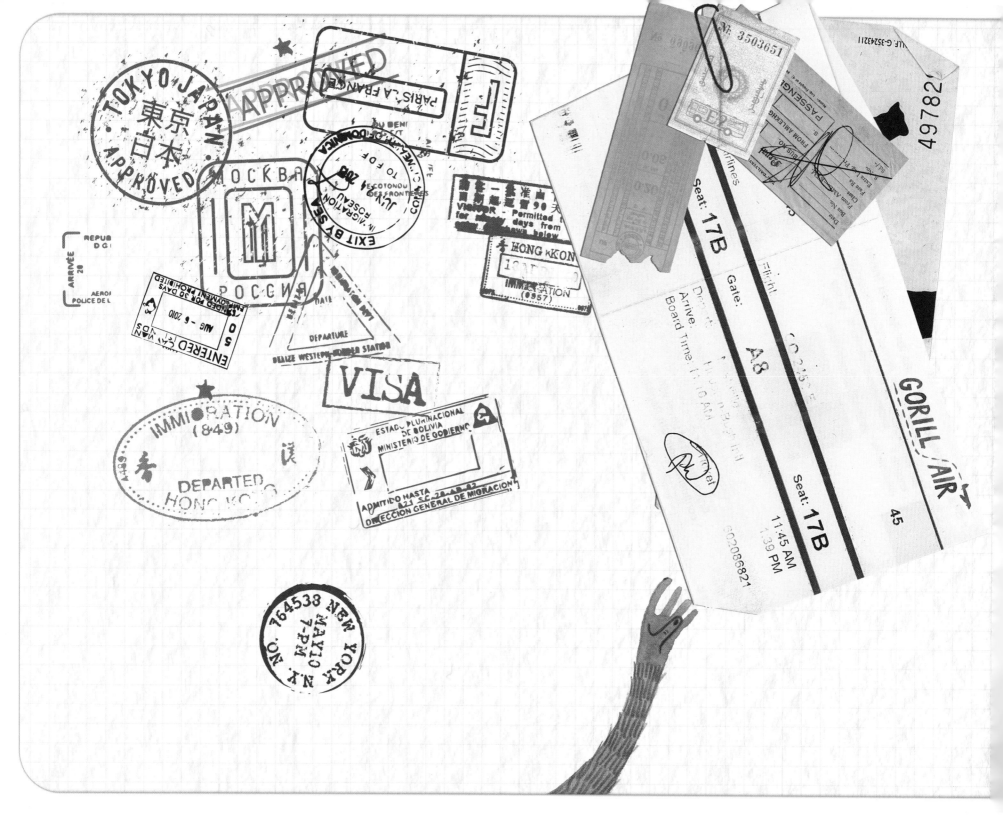

TOPIC OF STUDY:

PECULIAR PRIMATES

STUDY DESCRIPTION:

Fun Facts about These Curious Creatures

FIELD AUTHOR:

DEBRA KEMPF SHUMAKER

TRIP AUTHORIZED BY:

RP|KIDS
PHILADELPHIA

FIELD ARTIST:

CLAIRE POWELL

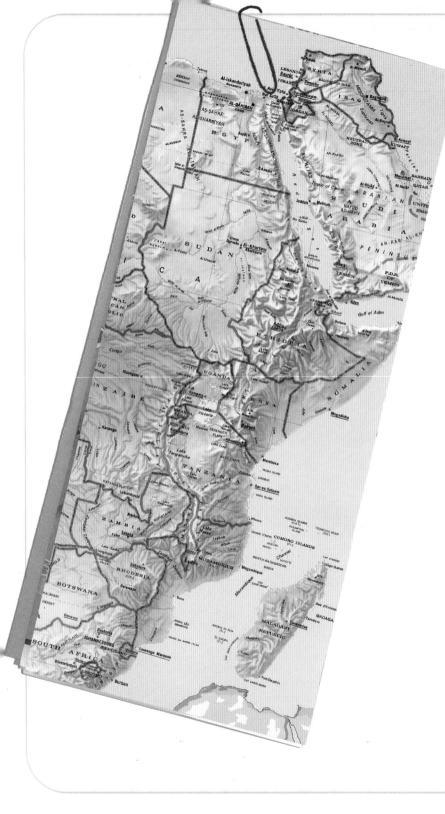

Running Press Kids
Hachette Book Group
1290 Avenue of the Americas, New York, NY 10104
www.runningpress.com/rpkids @RP_Kids

Printed in China

First Edition: October 2022

Published by Running Press Kids, an imprint of Perseus Books, LLC, a subsidiary of Hachette Book Group, Inc.
The Running Press Kids name and logo is a trademark of the Hachette Book Group.

The Hachette Speakers Bureau provides a wide range of authors for speaking events. To find out more, go to www.hachettespeakersbureau.com or call (866) 376-6591.

The publisher is not responsible for websites (or their content) that are not owned by the publisher.

Print book cover and interior design by Frances J. Soo Ping Chow.

Library of Congress Cataloging-in-Publication Data
Names: Shumaker, Debra Kempf, author. | Powell, Claire, illustrator. Title: Peculiar primates:
fun facts about these curious creatures / Debra Kempf Shumaker ; illustrated by Claire Powell.
Description: First edition. | Philadelphia : Running Press Kids, 2022. | Includes bibliographical references.
| Audience: Ages 4-8 | Identifiers: LCCN 2021032720 (print) | LCCN 2021032721 (ebook) |
ISBN 9780762478200 (hardcover) | ISBN 9780762478217 (ebook) | ISBN 9780762478231 (ebook)
| ISBN 9780762478255 (kindle edition) Subjects: LCSH: Primates—Juvenile literature. | Primates—
Behavior—Juvenile literature. Classification: LCC QL737.P9 K44 2022 (print) | LCC QL737.P9 (ebook) |
DDC 599.8—dc23 LC record available at https://lccn.loc.gov/2021032720 LC ebook record available
at https://lccn.loc.gov/2021032721

ISBNs: 978-0-7624-7820-0 (hardcover), 978-0-7624-7821-7 (ebook),
978-0-7624-7823-1 (ebook), 978-0-7624-7825-5 (ebook)

1010

10 9 8 7 6 5 4 3 2 1

Wish you were here!

To my parents, for providing

a house full of books.

-DKS

To Rachael, Tamsin

and Wild Beast;

3 cheeky monkeys.

-CP

All primates climb and breathe in air.

EMPEROR TAMARIN

SQUIRREL MONKEY

RING-TAILED LEMUR

They have big brains
and hands and hair.

HAMADRYAS BABOON

ORANGUTAN

SPIDER MONKEY

But...

some live alone,
some live in groups.

PECULIARITY DEPARTMENT RATING

7 / 10

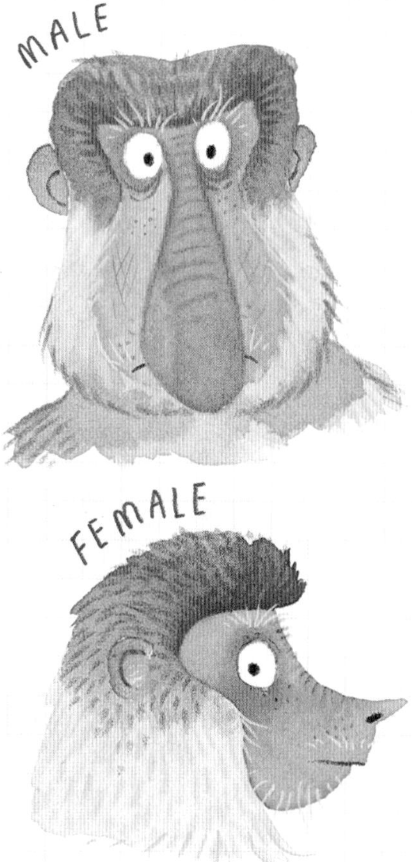

MALE

FEMALE

INCHES (NOT TO SCALE)

7

6

5

4

3

2

1

0

NOTE: FEMALE NOSE NOT AS ELONGATED AND TURNS SLIGHTLY UPWARD

One primate has a nose that droops.

Some primates hunt when it gets dark.

PRIMATE:	AYE-AYE
HABITAT:	MADAGASCAR
DIET:	WOOD-BORING BEETLE LARVAE
OBSERVATIONS:	

PECULIARITY DEPARTMENT RATING · $\frac{10}{10}$

WOOD-BORING BEETLE LARVAE

FIG 1: SKELETON OF HAND

One looks for food by tapping bark.

One's face is red,

another's blue.

PECULIARITY DEPARTMENT RATING

10/10

2/10

NAME: BALD UAKARI

NAME: GOLDEN SNUB-NOSED MONKEY

NAME: COTTON-TOP TAMARIN   NAME: HAMADRYAS BABOON

PECULIARITY DEPARTMENT RATING
7/10

Some primates sport
a fancy 'do.

One's butt is splashed with colored streaks.

SHY

CHEEK POUCHES TO STORE FOOD

LONG CANINE TEETH

WALKS ON ALL FOURS

MALE HAS A COLORFUL BUTT TO ATTRACT FEMALES

BUTTOCK PADS

ADULT MALE: 1.8—2.1 FT / ADULT FEMALE: 18—20 IN

ADULT MALE: 2.5—3.1 FT / ADULT FEMALE: 1.8—2.2 FT

MANDRILL

PECULIARITY RATING · PECULIARITY DEPARTMENT

10 / 10

PATAS

MANGABEY

Some primates store food in their cheeks.

MACAQUE

GUENON

ROYALTY SERIES Nº 12

NAMED AFTER A GERMAN EMPEROR.

One primate wears a cute mustache.

10 INCHES

LONG TONGUE

FROWN TO COMMUNICATE

CLAWS GRIP BARK

EMPEROR TAMARIN

TAIL GROWS 16 INCHES LONG

PECULIARITY DEPARTMENT RATING

6/10

Another likes
to soak and splash.

JAPANESE MACAQUE. HOT SPRINGS, NORTHERN JAPAN.

PECULIARITY DEPARTMENT RATING

6/10

GRASS

TREE NEEDLE

COCONUT FIBER

FEATHER

NICOBAR LONG-TAILED MACAQUES

Some primates floss
to keep teeth clean,

OCCUPIED

PECULIARITY DEPARTMENT · RATING ·

5/10

SPORTIVE LEMUR

while others use
the same latrine!

MALE
4–6 FEET

GORILLA

VERY BIG AND STRONG.
A CLOSE RELATIVE
TO US!

Some thump their chests
to show their might.

PECULIARITY DEPARTMENT RATING

5/10

Another has
a toxic bite.

· PECULIARITY DEPARTMENT RATING ·

$\frac{8}{10}$

A SLOW LORIS
FEELING THREATENED

+

OIL IN
ELBOW
GLAND

+

SALIVA
& TEETH

=

ACH WITH CAUTION

APPROACH WITH CAUTION

APPROACH WITH C

One primate has
a raucous howl.

HOWWWWL

HOWLER MONKEYS

PECULIARITY DEPARTMENT RATING
5/10

TARSIER

One turns   its head   just like   an owl!

Some primates build
a nest each night,

CHIMPANZEES
AND BONOBOS

Z z z z

TREE
CANOPY
=
SAFE

HUNGRY
PREDATOR

GROUND
=
NOT SAFE

PECULIARITY DEPARTMENT RATING

5 / 10

while others sleep
with tails twined tight.

Peculiar looks,
odd things they do.
Some primates can
be strange, it's true.

One walks and talks
and builds things, too.
That primate is—
yes—me and you!

WHO ARE THESE PECULIAR PRIMATES?

Primates, including humans, are mammals. There are more than 350 kinds of primates. All mammals have fur or hair, give birth, nurse their babies, care for their young, and breathe in air. But unlike other mammals, primates don't have paws. Instead, they have hands and feet, and most have opposable thumbs that allow them to grasp things. In addition, all primates can climb and most spend at least some of their time in trees.

PRIMATE WITH A NOSE THAT DROOPS: *Proboscis monkeys* live in the jungles of Borneo. The males have long, droopy noses that extend past their mouths and chins. Their noses are four to seven inches long! Scientists think the large size creates an echo chamber when the monkey calls, making the sound louder. This might impress the female monkeys and intimidate rival males.

PRIMATES THAT HUNT IN THE DARK: Most primates are active in the day and sleep at night. However, several *families* of primates are actually nocturnal, including *pottos*, *golagos*, *dwarf lemurs*, *slow lorises*, *tarsiers*, *mouse lemurs*, *night monkeys*, and a few more. These primates have very large eyes that allow them to hunt at night.

PRIMATE THAT LOOKS FOR FOOD BY TAPPING BARK: The *aye-aye* lives on the island of Madagascar. Part of its diet is the larvae of the wood-boring beetle that is found in tree branches. To find this larvae, the aye-aye uses its long middle finger to tap on the bark of the tree, listening for hollow cavities in the wood where larvae might be hiding. When it finds a cavity, it bites down on the branch, then uses that finger to dig out any larvae.

PRIMATE THAT HAS A RED FACE: The *bald uakari* lives in the Amazon rainforests of Peru and Brazil. Its face is bright red because of a high concentration of blood vessels under a thin layer of skin. The healthier the monkey, the redder the face!

PRIMATE WITH A BLUE FACE: Though the *golden snub-nosed monkey* is named for its thick, golden hair and flat nose, the pale blue skin around its eyes is striking, too. These monkeys live in the mountain forests of China, which can be covered with snow for several months each year. Scientists think their flat noses protect them from frostbite.

PRIMATES THAT SPORT A FANCY 'DO: *Cotton-top tamarins* are small, squirrel-sized monkeys that live in the tropical forests of Colombia in South America. They have a halo of soft, white hair around their gray and silver faces. When threatened, they raise and lower this "'do" to appear larger.

Male *hamadryas baboons* also have fancy hairstyles, with a long, silvery mane around their head and on their shoulders. Hamadryas baboons live in northeast Africa, Saudi Arabia, and Yemen.

PRIMATE WHOSE BUTT IS SPLASHED WITH COLORED STREAKS: The *mandrills* are the world's largest monkey, and they live on the west coast of Central Africa. Male mandrills have bright blue, red, and purple streaks on their faces and their butts to attract females. When they are excited, the colors on their bottoms become even brighter.

PRIMATES THAT STORE FOOD IN THEIR CHEEKS: Old World monkeys (monkeys that live in Asia and Africa), like the *baboons*, *mangabeys*, *mandrills*, *guenons*, *patas*, and *macaques* have cheek pouches that can stretch down to their necks. When these monkeys are searching for food and are disturbed by predators or other monkeys, they stuff their cheeks and run away on all four limbs to trees or rocks. Once safe, they eat their stored food.

PRIMATE THAT WEARS A CUTE MUSTACHE: The *emperor tamarin* is a small, squirrel-sized monkey that lives in the Amazon rainforests of Brazil and the northeast corner of Bolivia. Its long, white whiskers curl down, resembling a large mustache. The emperor tamarin was named after the German Emperor Wilhelm II, who sported a similar long, white mustache.

PRIMATE THAT LIKES TO SOAK AND SPLASH: The *Japanese macaques*, also known as *snow monkeys*, live in the northern regions of Japanese mountains and highlands where it snows in the winter. To get warm, the monkeys soak in the hot springs and thermal pools heated by nearby volcanoes. Some just sit and soak. Some splash around and scrub each other. They like baths so much, the Japanese government designated some hot springs just for them!

PRIMATES THAT FLOSS THEIR TEETH CLEAN: *Nicobar long-tailed macaques* on the Great Nicobar Island in the Indian ocean enjoy eating thorny, slimy, and hairy food. Several of them have been observed using tree needles, bird feathers, coconut fibers, and blades of grass to clean out dirt between their teeth after they eat! Other types of macaques floss, too. Even baboons in an English zoo have been seen using hair or old broom bristles to clean their teeth.

PRIMATES THAT USE THE SAME LATRINE: While they don't have actual houses with bathrooms, some lemurs, like the *sportive lemur*, do use a common spot to pee and poop . . . and leave each other messages! Though these lemurs live in parent/offspring groups, they are solitary and prefer not to interact with each other. At night, these lemurs will use their common latrine at different times, but since each lemur's pee is unique, they "check in" with each other through their pee odor. Lemur pee can even warn other males to stay away. Lemurs live on Madagascar.

PRIMATES THAT THUMP THEIR CHESTS TO SHOW THEIR MIGHT

: *Gorillas*, the largest apes, live in tropical forests near the equator in Africa. Though they are robust and powerful, gorillas are typically unaggressive unless they feel danger. To defend their family group, the lead male gorilla will stand upright, beat his chest, cry out, then charge.

PRIMATE WITH A TOXIC BITE

: The *slow loris* lives in South and Southeast Asia and is the only venomous primate in the world. But its venom glands are not in its mouth. Instead, they're near its elbows! To give a poisonous bite, the slow loris first stretches out its arm to activate the gland. Then it licks its arm to mix the toxin with its saliva before it bites its victim. The toxin can cause an allergic reaction and even death. It's also possible that a mother will spread the poison on her babies to protect them from predators while she goes foraging.

PRIMATE WITH A RAUCOUS HOWL

: While many monkeys and apes have boisterous calls and morning choruses, the *howler monkeys* of South America are the loudest of the primates. Howler monkeys have special inflatable sacs and unusually large bones in their throats that make the calls extra loud—a male can be heard two to three miles away! Why do they call so loudly? They are likely announcing themselves and claiming their treetop territory.

PRIMATE THAT TURNS ITS HEAD LIKE AN OWL

: *Tarsiers* are primates that live on islands of Southeast Asia. They are nocturnal primates and have very large eyes, which can't move. To look in different directions, they must move their entire head. Fortunately, their spine is formed in such a way that they can turn their head 180 degrees each way—the farthest of any mammal—and almost as far as owls can turn their heads.

PRIMATES THAT BUILD A NEST EACH NIGHT

: Most great apes—*bonobos*, *chimpanzees*, *gorillas*, and *orangutans*—build nests each night before they go to sleep. Many of these nests are built up in trees. The apes find horizontal branches and bend and break other branches to build up a rim. Sometimes they will even weave those branches in! Nests can be in one tree or connect to several trees. Just like bird nests, the primate nests are oval or circular. Unlike birds, however, primates build new nests each night!

PRIMATES THAT SLEEP WITH TAILS TWINED TIGHT

: *Titi monkeys* live in the trees of the Amazon forests in Brazil. Males and females create a bond and like to be close to each other throughout the day, frequently twining their tails together to reinforce that special bond. Sometimes, they even sleep with their tails entwined!

Thank you to Debra Curtin with the New England Primate Conservancy
for reviewing the facts in this book.

FURTHER LEARNING:

WEBSITES:

New England Primate Conservancy raises awareness about the needs for primate protection, both for those in captivity and in the wild. Since 69% of primate species are threatened by extinction, to protect them the Primate Conservancy hopes that education will inspire everyone to do more. https://www.neprimateconservancy.org/

BOOKS:

Aye-ayes, Nocturnal Animals Series by Kristin Petrie. ABDO Publishing, 2010.

Lemurs, Amazing Animals Series by Valerie Bodden. Creative Education, 2019.

Monkeys and Other Primates, A Bobbie Kalman Book by Rebecca Sjonger and Bobbie Kalman. Crabtree Publishing, 2005.

Nature's Children, New World Monkeys by Amanda Harman. Grolier Educational, Danbury, CT. 2001

Tarsiers, Nocturnal Animals Series by Kristin Petrie. ABDO Publishing, 2010.

VIDEOS:

Chimpanzee building a nest: https://www.youtube.com/watch?v=JM9zZW7HdF0

Monkey flossing its teeth with a bird feather:
https://www.newscientist.com/article/2152868-watch-a-monkey-floss-its-teeth-with-a-bird-feather/

SELECTED SOURCES

Armstrong, David. "No monkeys like snow monkeys: Soak up Japan's hot-tubbing wildlife."
https://www.sfgate.com/travel/article/No-monkeys-like-snow-monkeys-Soak-up-Japan-s-3292583.php. Accessed 3 January 2020.

Curtin, Debra. Emails to author, January 2020, December 2020.

Dell'Amore, Christine. "Venomous Primate Discovered in Borneo."
https://www.nationalgeographic.com/news/2012/12/venomous-primate-discovered-in-borneo/.
15 December 2012. Accessed 17 September 2019.

Fox-Skelly, Jasmin. "Zoologger: Shy lemurs communicate using toilet trees."
https://www.newscientist.com/article/dn26392-zoologger-shy-lemurs-communicate-using-toilet-trees/.
16 October 2014. Accessed 4 January 2020.

"Gorilla." Encyclopedia Brittanica online. https://www.britannica.com/animal/Gorilla-primate-genus.
25 October 2016. Accessed 4 January 2020.

Gron KJ. Primate Factsheets: Aye-aye (*Daubentonia madagascariensis*) Taxonomy, Morphology, & Ecology.
http://pin.primate.wisc.edu/factsheets/entry/aye-aye. 2007 July 27. Accessed 5 December 2019.

Hayden, Nancy. "List of Nocturnal Primates." https://animals.mom.me/list-of-nocturnal-primates-7842751.html.
01 November 2017. Accessed 02 December 2019.

Laberge, Maxine. "Chimps, Humans, and Monkeys: What's the Difference?"
https://news.janegoodall.org/2018/06/27/chimps-humans-monkeys-whats-difference/. 27 June 2018. Accessed 22 January 2020.

O'Neil, Dennis. "The Primates: Old World Monkeys." https://www2.palomar.edu/anthro/primate/prim_6.htm.
Copyright 1998 - 2014. Accessed 3 January 2020.

"Primate Facts." https://www.neprimateconservancy.org/primate-facts.html. Accessed 11 January 2020.

"Primate Species Profiles." https://www.neprimateconservancy.org/primate-profiles.html/.
Accessed January 2020.

"Why do baboons floss?" University of Exeter Biosciences News online.
https://biosciences.exeter.ac.uk/news/articles/whydobaboonsfloss.html. 3 September 2018. Accessed 4 January 2020.

A complete bibliography is available on the author's website
www.debrashumaker.com.

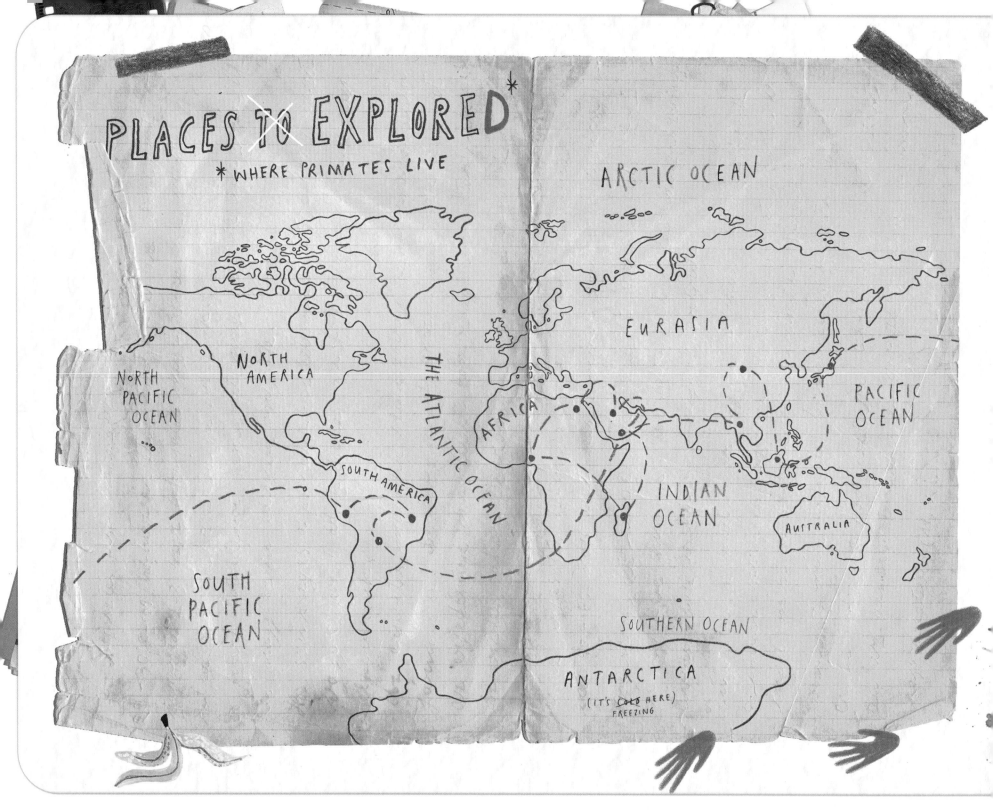